HAL•LEONARD
Beginning
PIANOSOLO
PLAY-ALONG

Christmas CLASSICS

CONTENTS

Page	Title	Demo Track	Play-Along Track
2	The First Noel	1	2
4	Jingle Bells	3	4
6	Joy to the World	5	6
8	O Come, All Ye Faithful	7	8
10	Silent Night	9	10
16	Up on the Housetop	15	16
12	We Wish You a Merry Christmas	11	12
14	What Child Is This?	13	14

ISBN 978-1-4584-0829-7

HAL•LEONARD®
CORPORATION
7777 W. BLUEMOUND RD. P.O. BOX 13819 MILWAUKEE, WI 53213

In Australia Contact:
Hal Leonard Australia Pty. Ltd.
4 Lentara Court
Cheltenham, Victoria, 3192 Australia
Email: ausadmin@halleonard.com.au

Visit Hal Leonard Online at
www.halleonard.com

THE FIRST NOEL

17th Century English Carol
Music from W. Sandys' *Christmas Carols*

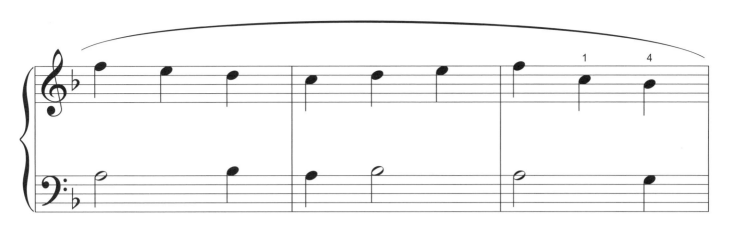

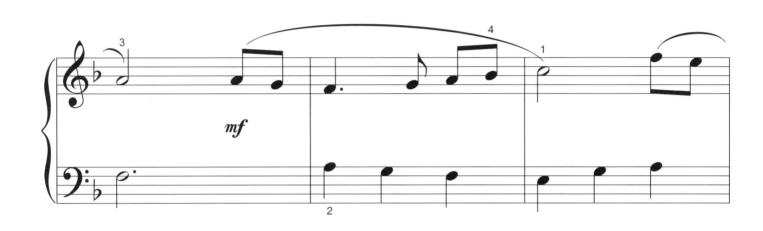

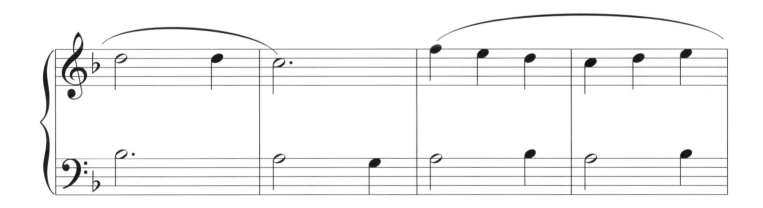

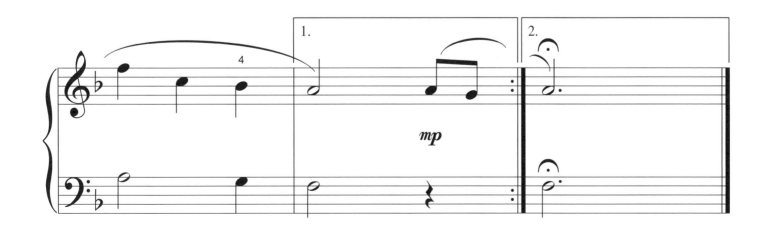

JINGLE BELLS

Words and Music by
J. PIERPONT

With spirit

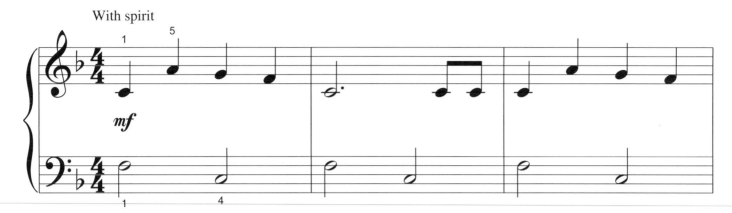

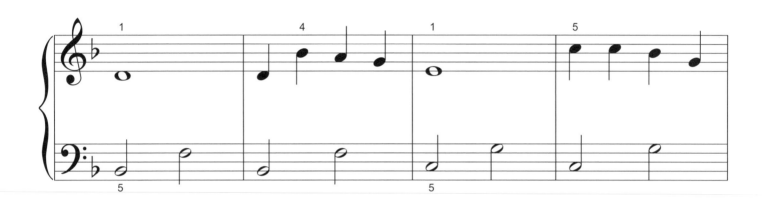

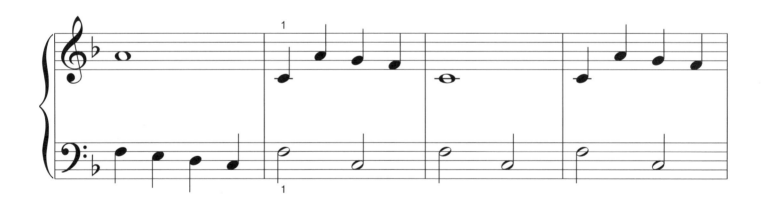

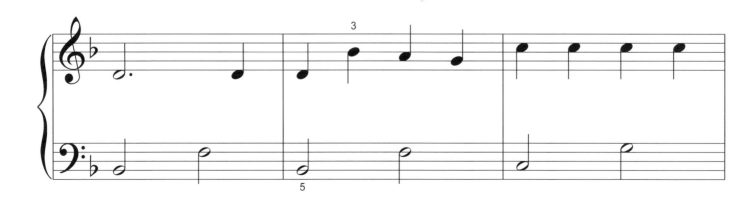

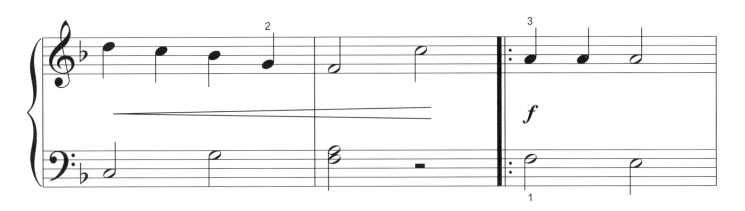

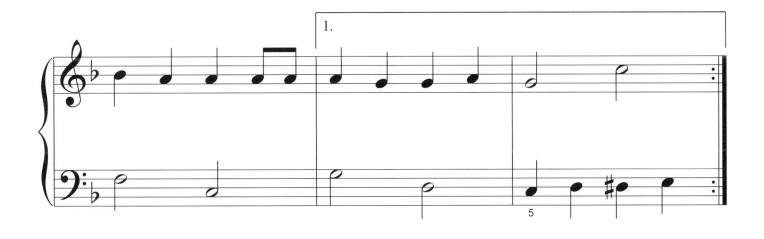

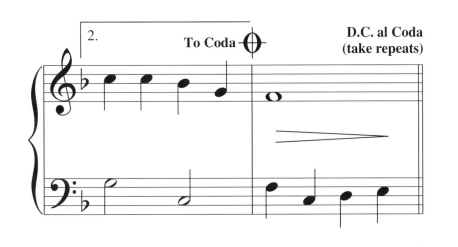

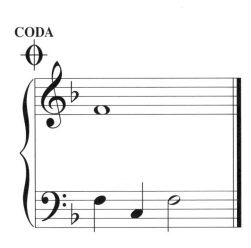

JOY TO THE WORLD

Words by ISAAC WATTS
Music by GEORGE FRIDERIC HANDEL
Adapted by LOWELL MASON

With spirit

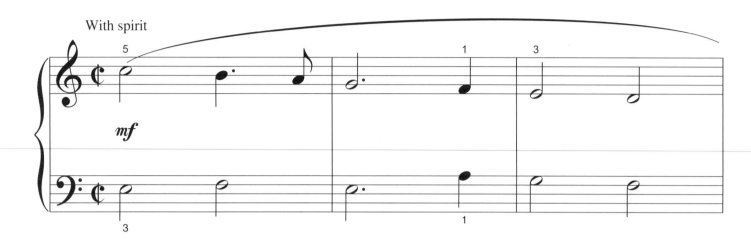

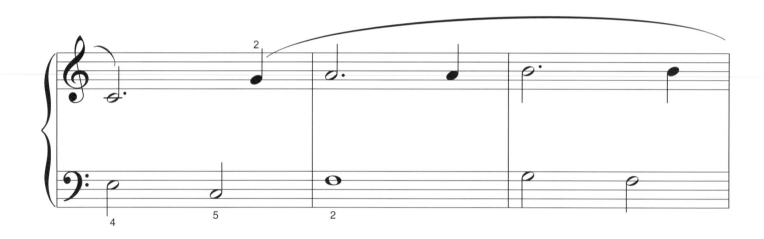

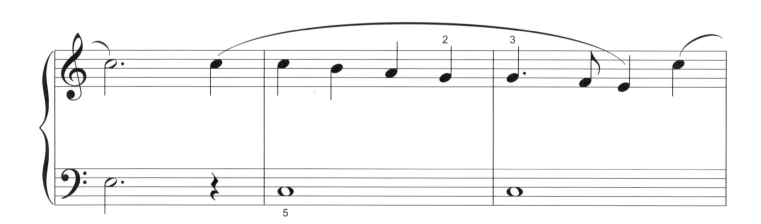

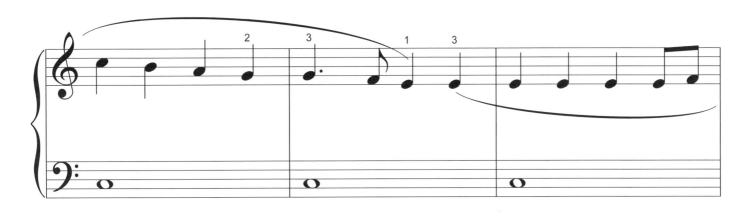

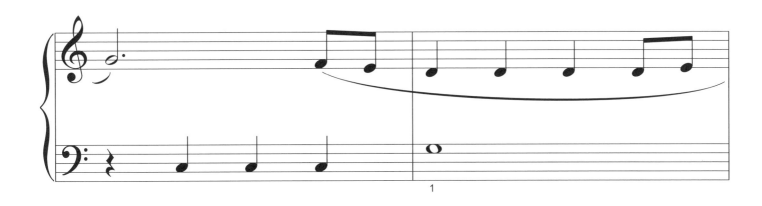

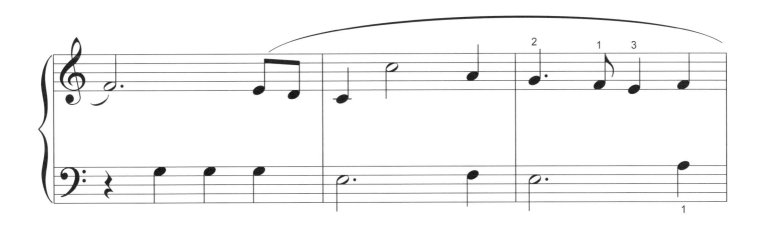

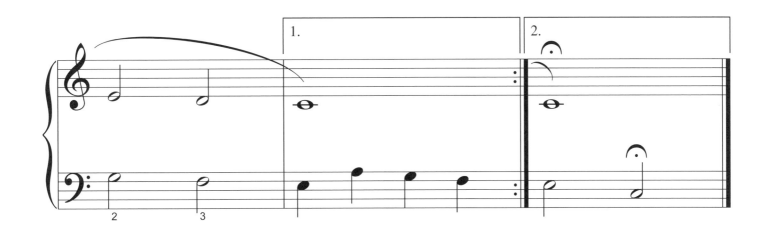

O COME, ALL YE FAITHFUL
(Adeste Fideles)

Music by JOHN FRANCIS WADE
Latin Words translated by FREDERICK OAKELEY

Triumphantly

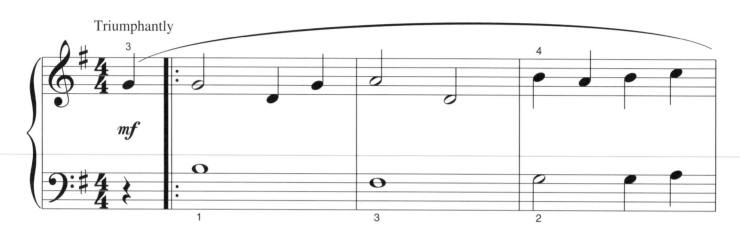

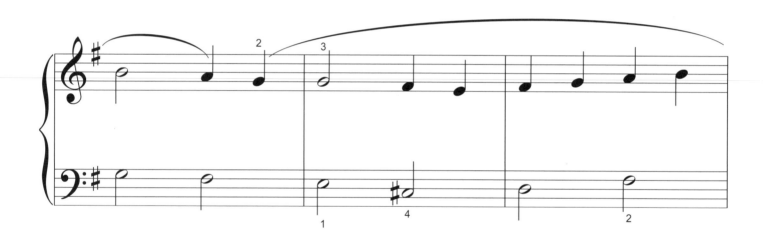

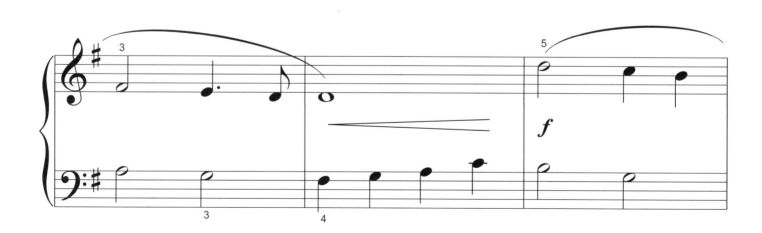

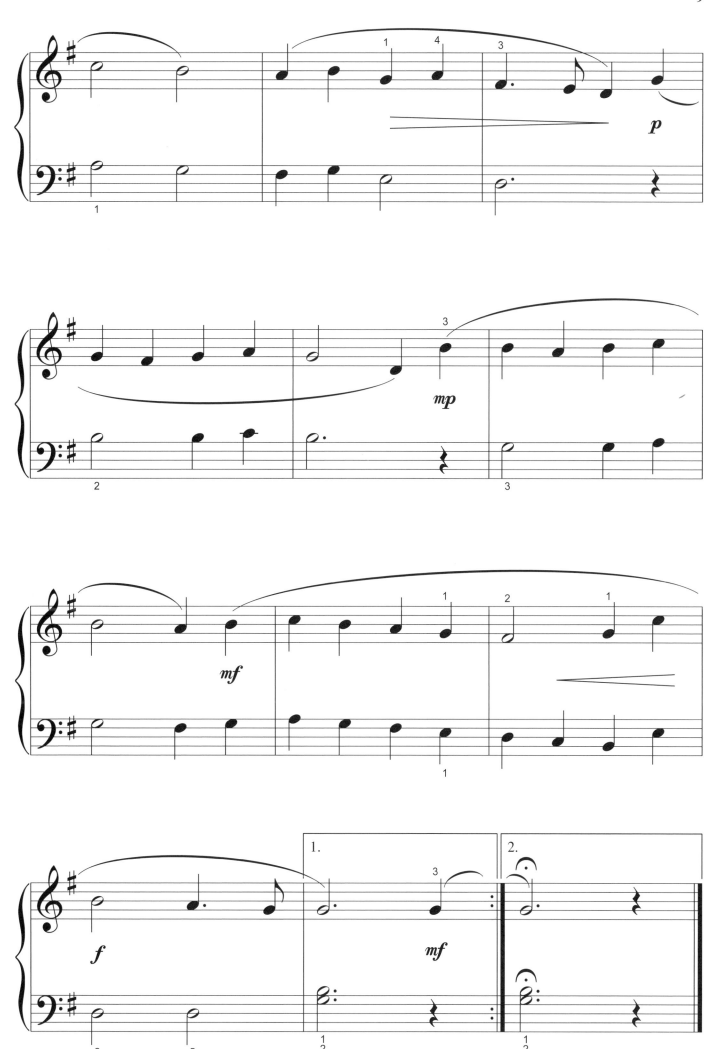

SILENT NIGHT

Words by JOSEPH MOHR
Translated by JOHN F. YOUNG
Music by FRANZ X. GRUBER

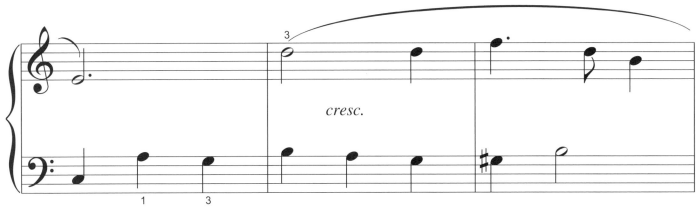

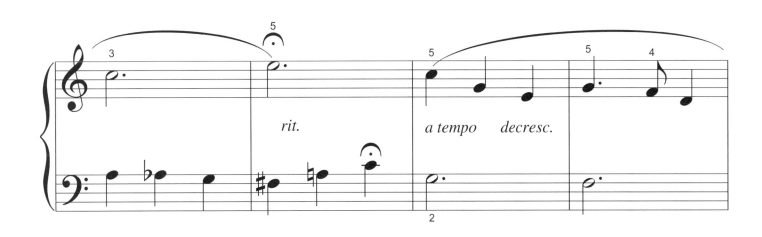

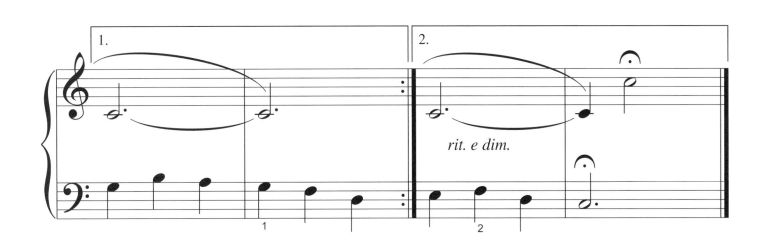

WE WISH YOU A MERRY CHRISTMAS

Traditional English Folksong

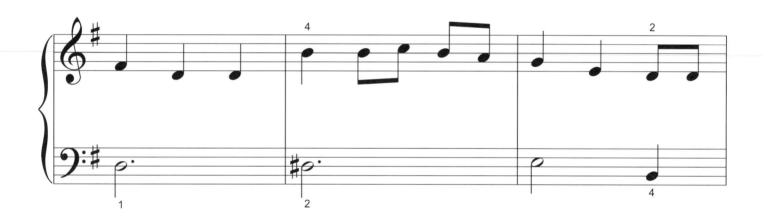

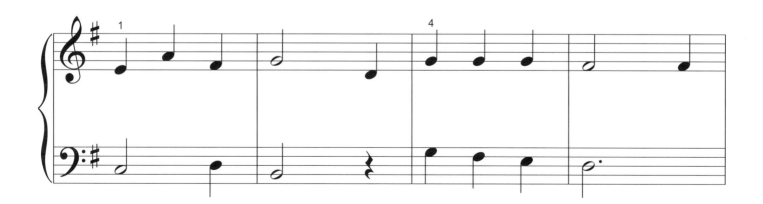

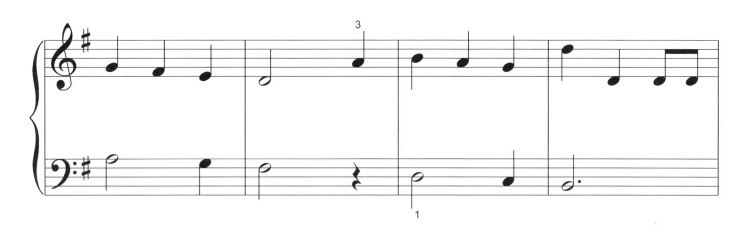

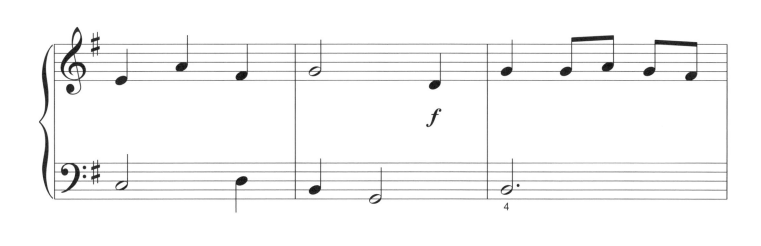

WHAT CHILD IS THIS?

Words by WILLIAM C. DIX
16th Century English Melody

UP ON THE HOUSETOP

Words and Music by
B.R. HANBY

Brightly, with a swing

mf–f

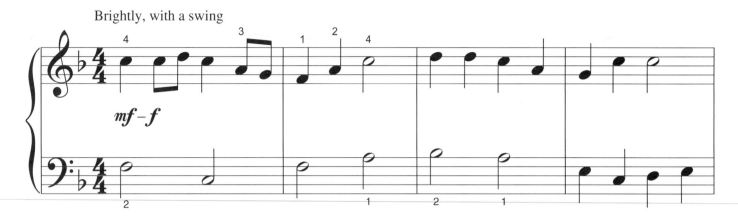

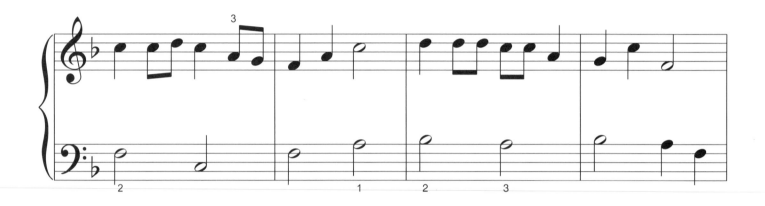